MY SUPERDAD

by Michael Gordon

THIS BOOK BELONGS TO

....

....

Davy knows he's a very
lucky little guy;

His dad is a superhero,
although he can't fly.

But he does many other
superhero-type tasks;

In fact, he can do most
anything Davy asks.

When Dad comes home from
work at the end of the day,

No matter how tired, he
still has time to play.

He shows his powers when
making Davy's dinner;

He chops veggies for soup like
a souperhuman winner.

He has x-ray vision—he sees
inside Davy's head;

He knows exactly when
Davy is ready for bed.

Davy challenges him to guess
what book he should read;

His dad always gets it right;
he's a mind reader, indeed.

Whenever Davy needs his
dad, his dad will appear;

He seems to be in two places
at once, both far and near.

One minute in the yard, and
the next in the hall,

When Davy needs his dad,
he just has to call.

But before he can shout, his
dad's already there;

When asked how he does it,
Dad says he won't share.

"Superheroes don't talk about
their powers," he'll say,

"But, since you're my favorite,
I'll tell you one day."

When Davy doesn't feel
well, his dad is the best

At taking his mind off his
illness so he can rest.

He's always able to make
Davy feel fine.

With fun and laughter, he's
better in no time.

There's nothing Davy's dad
can't fix, he's good at it all;

From bikes and broken toys
to a deflated ball.

Whenever something needs
repair, "I'll fix it," he'll say;

Davy knows he can depend
on his dad every day.

When Davy and Teddy are
scared in bed all alone,

They have a monster-fighting
hero of their very own.

He uses x-ray vision to
see invisible slime;

Davy's dad can make monsters
disappear every time.

He hunts down the monster and shouts, "Monster be gone!"

So Davy doesn't have to sleep with the bedroom light on.

When he's reading a story, he keeps his eyes ready,

To spot any new monsters set to scare Davy and Teddy.

Davy's dad is a hero—the
best kind, it's true;

Better than those on TV, he's
super through and through.

Dad says, "I love you, Davy,
I'm lucky you're my son."

"I love you too, Dad," says Davy,
"I think I'm the lucky one."

About author

Michael Gordon is the talented author of several highly rated children's books including the popular Sleep Tight, Little Monster, and the Animal Bedtime.

He collaborates with the renowned Kids Book Book that creates picture books for all of ages to enjoy. Michael's goal is to create books that are engaging, funny, and inspirational for children of all ages and their parents.

Contact

For all other questions about books or author, please e-mail michaelgordonclub@gmail.com.

Award-winning books

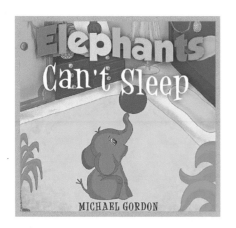

Elephants Can not Sleep

The

Little Elephant likes to break the rules. He never cleans his room. He never listens to mama's bedtime stories and goes to bed really late. But what if he tried to follow the routine so that the bedtime would become an amazing experience?

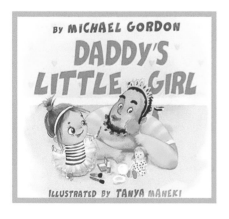

Little Girl's Daddy

the Who Needs a super hero the when you have your dad? Written in beautiful rhyme this is an excellent story that honors all fathers in the world.

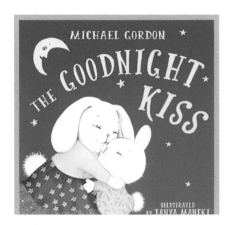

The Goodnight Kiss

Welcome to a cozy, sweet little bunny family. Mom is putting her little son Ben to bed, but she's not quite successful. Little boy still wants to play games and stay up late. Ben also likes to keep his mommy in his room at bedtime. Mrs. Bunny tries milk, warm blankets, books , and finally a kiss ... what will work?

My Big Brother

The

Each of our lives will always be a special part of the other.
There's Nothing Quite Like A Sibling Bond Written in beautiful rhyme this is an excellent story that values patience, acceptance and bond between a brother and his sister.

Thank You!

For purchasing this book,

I'd like to give you a free gift

An amazing bedtime story for your child

https://michaelgordonclub.wixsite.com/books

CPSIA information can be obtained
at www.ICGtesting.com
Printed in the USA
LVHW072306200522
719346LV00002B/74